ECK Wisdom
on
Inner
Guidance

ECK Wisdom

on

Inner
Guidance

HAROLD KLEMP

ECKANKAR
Minneapolis
Eckankar.org

ECK Wisdom on Inner Guidance

Copyright © 2016 ECKANKAR

Printed in USA

Photo of Sri Harold Klemp (page 76)
by Art Galbraith

Second printing—2023

Library of Congress Cataloging-in-Publication Data

Names: Klemp, Harold, author.
Title: ECK wisdom on inner guidance / Harold Klemp, EK.
Description: Minneapolis : Eckankar, 2016.
Identifiers: LCCN 2016002906 | ISBN 9781570434129 (pbk. : alk. paper)
Subjects: LCSH: Spiritual life--Eckankar (Organization) | Eckankar (Organization)--Doctrines.
Classification: LCC BP605.E3 K55385 2016 | DDC 299/.93--dc23
LC record available at http://lccn.loc.gov/2016002906

♾ This paper meets the requirements of ANSI/NISO Z39.48-1992 (Permanence of Paper).

My definition of a true religion is one that does good in the world.

It tries to find ways to help people be themselves. It does not try to shape people to be what we think they should be, then break spiritual or man-made laws to accomplish that. The sign of a good religion is that it helps the people grow to become more godlike, to be capable of more love and mercy—for themselves as well as for others.

—Harold Klemp

Contents

FRED AND THE LOST FILE

*F*red wasn't an ECKist, a member of ECK, but he married one. And he told of an experience that convinced him there was something to Eckankar, HU, Soul Travel, and the Spiritual Eye. He and his wife live in Canada. His wife had come from Germany, and after they'd settled in Canada, they decided to go back to Germany and pack up her belongings.

So they made the trip. They packed everything in boxes, and his wife told Fred, "You take care of everything in the office and mark the boxes *Office*; take care of the files and whatever else you find."

Fred went to the office and packed everything up. In a front room, there were soon

1

rows and rows of boxes stacked to the ceiling. After they'd been at this for most of the day, Fred's wife asked if he had happened to see a certain file. "I need that file," she said.

Fred said, "I don't know anything about the files. You just said to pack them; I didn't read them."

"We're just going to have to find that file," she said.

The office boxes were mixed with the rest of the boxes, so as they had time, Fred and his wife pulled boxes down and looked. But they couldn't find the file.

The night before the moving company was going to come, Fred's wife said, "I know how we can find it."

It was late, and he was so tired. He said, "How?"

She said, "Come in here to the couch. We'll sit down and do a contemplation."

He said, "What?" She hadn't talked to

him too much about contemplation.

She said, "We'll sing *HU*."

Fred had heard about HU, the holy name for God, only once before. But he was too tired to argue. He sat down on the couch with his wife. She said, "Put your attention at the Spiritual Eye, which is back in the center of your head, right about here." She touched the place between her eyebrows.

As they sang *HU*, Fred felt a slight pressure there. Then suddenly, just as clearly as a slide projector throwing a picture up on a white screen, he saw the box. He saw the row, and he saw where it was in the row. They came out of contemplation, and he said to his wife, "I know where the box is."

They went into the room. The box was in the second row, third box back from the wall, at a certain height. They had to dig. Fred said, "And you'll find that the file is upside down in the box. That's why you couldn't find it."

They looked in the box, and Fred's wife pulled out a file that was upside down. It was the very file they had been looking for. They were both astounded—even the wife, the ECKist who knew all about HU.

At first Fred thought, *Maybe this was just something in my subconscious mind.* "That's where it was, dear," he said. "It was in my subconscious mind."

His wife said, "But you didn't open the file. You didn't even know what it was."

Fred said, "That's right. You're right, dear." What's a husband to say?

But this experience got Fred thinking. His wife had told him about Soul Travel and Eckankar. Maybe there was something to it.

Maybe there was a place in his life for inner guidance.

SOUL—A SPARK OF GOD

*O*ften people are afraid to follow their inner guidance. It sounds like such a foolish thing to do, especially if they have to face other people and explain why they are doing what they are doing.

One of the very strong pressures in life is the social consciousness: What will people think? What will people say?

The social consciousness is so strong that it keeps people in religions that they have outgrown years ago. But they're afraid to leave because they worry about what the neighbors will say. It is a very strong force that the negative power uses to keep people in line.

It keeps them trapped in their present life, in their state of futility, in their state of hopelessness and unhappiness. Most people do not have the spiritual strength to muster the courage to take a step away from the crowd.

Yet showers of love rain down upon us simply because we are Soul, a divine spark of God. Its Voice, which showers the love, is the pure Light and Sound.

The Creator, the Highest Being, speaks to creation through the Holy Spirit, the ECK. This voice of divine love is very real.

Those who enter the higher reaches of heaven here and now in their states of consciousness see the holy Light and hear the divine Sound of God clearly in everyday life.

The Light and Sound are God's way to communicate directly with us. They help develop our creativity, which makes us godlike.

Key to the
Door of Truth

How ow do *you* recognize truth?

Most people respond to the Light and Sound of God indirectly by listening to their intuition, trusting their feelings, or following their conscience.

But others do see the Light directly; It often appears before the Sound. They are two parts of the Voice of God, the ECK, which speaks to all whose spiritual eyes can see the mysteries of divine love.

Each of us is a unique individual, with our own peculiar combination of experiences accumulated over many lifetimes. The truth of ECK comes to each of us like a special key, custom-designed with millions of little notches and grooves. It is the only key that will fit the lock, turn it, and open the door of Soul.

You can pick up the inspiration to find this key for yourself. If you can take the inspiration into contemplation, you can build the spiritual strength and understanding to accept the ECK, the Holy Spirit, as It speaks to you every moment of every day.

The ways in which the ECK works are limitless.

A Simple Request

If you're unhappy, open yourself to the possibility that there is something better.

If you're an ECKist say, "MAHANTA,* please show me thy ways. Show me what may be there for me."

---

* Inner spiritual guide. See pages 14–18 for more information.

If you're Christian or Jewish or of any other faith, look to the God of your faith. Look to your savior, look to your way of spirituality, and ask, "Show me truth, God."

If you're sincere, God's Voice, the Holy Spirit, will begin opening you to truth.

BLUE-LIGHT BLESSING

$\mathcal{T}$om calls New York City home and lives there with his family. He'd been feeling a real concern for the safety of his loved ones because of runaway street crime and the drug problem. Such things are commonplace in his neighborhood.

His mother, June, is a pious Catholic. She knew next to nothing about Eckankar and showed even less inclination to learn about it.

Of course, Tom worried about her safety as well as that of other relatives living in the area. So he talked to the MAHANTA, his inner spiritual guide. In his conversation with the MAHANTA, Tom said, "If it's OK and I'm not interfering in my mother's space, is there some way to provide protection for her?"

About the same time he was talking with the MAHANTA, June was praying at home. She'd felt a real dread of becoming a crime victim. So, in her prayer she pleaded, "God, please send me a guardian angel."

A short time later, as she sat in her living room, a beautiful blue light appeared.

ECKists refer to it as the Blue Light of the MAHANTA. The MAHANTA, or Inner Master, is the highest state of consciousness known to the chronicles of mankind, and this blue light often appears during contemplation. It tells of the presence of the MAHANTA.

The Blue Light makes no distinctions between religions. People in religions other than Eckankar sometimes speak of it, too, but without understanding its nature. However, they do sense that the Blue Light comes to render a blessing—to give consolation to the heart, assurance to the spirit, and healing to the body.

The Blue Light of the MAHANTA is, then, one of countless ways the Inner Master may show up and pass along the assurance of protection.

When June fell asleep that night—and remember, she knew next to nothing about Eckankar but its name—she had a dream. In it she felt a strong, unfamiliar urging. She later said, "I had to sing *HU*."

HU is a love song to God that ECKists like to sing as a spiritual exercise. It's a very old name for God familiar to many cultures. The word helps open the heart and spread its wings like a dove. "To open your wings" means to open your state of consciousness, like a blooming rose.

This is what June saw in her dream: a bright light wrapped itself around her, as light and airy as chiffon. It was the very same kind of blue light that had so startled her in the living room. Back then, when she'd told Tom of the light, he pointed to the spiritual tie-in between the Blue Light and the Inner Master.

The dream lent June full assurance that God had indeed sent a guardian angel in answer to her prayer.

THE MAHANTA SERVES AS AN INNER GUIDE

*W*ho and what is the MAHANTA, the Living ECK Master in Eckankar? What is his function?

The MAHANTA, the Living ECK Master is the spiritual leader of Eckankar. He is the spiritual guide for those on the path of ECK.

Sometimes people don't understand the role of a spiritual guide—whether it's Christ or the MAHANTA or Buddha or the leader of a church somewhere who has a very definite, direct connection with the Holy Spirit.

So let me explain.

Over all creation is the Creator, God,

whom we know as SUGMAD in the ancient teachings. The name doesn't make any difference. The Creator is one and the same.

The Voice of God, the ECK, is the active force that goes out and is responsible for the actual creation of all the universes. This Voice of God is what is known as the Holy Spirit. Or sometimes the Spirit of God, the creative force, or whatever. But it's a neutral force. It simply obeys or does the will of the Creator.

A True Spiritual Master

A true spiritual master is in tune with the Voice of God. A human manifestation that people can see and understand. In that role, his will is that of Divine Spirit. And that's all.

In Eckankar this divine force works both in the Outer Master and through the Inner Master.

That means those on the path of ECK have the additional benefit of a Master who can come to them in the dream state and teach them there. Or sometimes by direct Soul Travel. Sometimes through contemplation. The Inner Master is there, working when the individual sleeps or prays or meditates or contemplates. And the Outer Master is out here to provide the books and discourses, and to give talks and things of this nature.

But the Outer and Inner Master are not two separate things; they're just two different aspects of one being who serves the Holy Spirit.

In his physical body, the MAHANTA, the Living ECK Master is like everyone else and can only be in one place at a time. In the Soul body, however, he is like the air that you breathe. He is everywhere. As the ECK, he can easily be with you and thousands of others in the very same moment.

The sole purpose of the MAHANTA, the Living ECK Master is simply to help Soul find Its way home to God.

Spiritual Help Is at Hand

As we step further along the path to self-mastership, we work with this ECK as It manifests to us and gives us direction. It will be different for everyone.

Some will see the Inner Master come and give them hints and directions. Others will feel gentle nudgings. If it's a matter of health, or of refilling the wallet and trying to figure out how to get the business going again, the ECK will give nudges. As we do the Spiritual Exercises of ECK, our consciousness opens. We become more aware of the help that is already at hand.

Spiritual exercises link you with the guidance of the Holy Spirit, which is seen as Light and heard as Sound. The inner Sound is the Voice of God calling us home. The inner Light is a beacon to light our way. All the Spiritual Exercises of ECK are built on these two divine aspects of the Holy Spirit.

Learning spiritual consciousness is

learning how to live in this world no matter what comes. We learn through these spiritual exercises how to live life graciously, from childhood to old age.

We learn how to live life in the best way possible.

A SPIRITUAL EXERCISE
TO LISTEN FOR GOD

*T*ry this simple spiritual exercise to help you hear and see the two aspects of God, the Light and Sound.

Go somewhere quiet. Sit or lie down in a comfortable place. Put your attention on your Spiritual Eye, a point just above and behind your eyebrows. With eyes lightly shut, begin to sing a holy word or phrase, such as *HU*, *God*, *Holy Spirit*, or *Show me thy ways, O Lord*. But fill your heart with love before you approach the altar of God, because only the pure may come.

Be patient. Do this exercise daily for several weeks, for a limit of twenty minutes each time. Sit, sing, and wait. God speaks to you only when you are able to listen.

GiftofHU.org

Scan to learn more about HU.

Dream Guidance Opens the Door to a Miracle

Some years ago, doctors told Rebecca that she was barren—she would never have children. She's a member of Eckankar and has come to believe in her dreams. Despite this prognosis by the doctors, she still wanted to be a mother, to have her own children. So she opened herself to the ECK and said, "If there's any way for me to have my own children, please let it be so."

She determined at this time that she would begin living her religion. So as a member of Eckankar, she began to do her spiritual exercises every day. She read a lot of ECK books, and she practiced the ECK principles as best she could.

What was she doing? She was spiritualizing herself.

She was doing everything possible to put the most positive light on everything in her life so that it would uplift her, because she knew that then the power of God can get through more easily.

One time, Rebecca did a spiritual exercise which she felt would help. She used a visualization technique in contemplation. She was trying to imagine herself in a place of healing.

She awoke in a dream and found herself in a large hospital on a higher level of existence. A doctor examined her, took her into the operating room, and operated on her. After it was over and she was about to be discharged, the doctor handed her a prescription. He told her the name of the medicine, and she memorized it.

Just at the moment the doctor mentioned the medicine, she felt this movement in her lower abdomen. Something moved inside her. Then she awoke.

She wrote down the dream in her dream journal. On a separate piece of paper she wrote the name of the medicine. Then she went back to sleep.

Next morning she got up and began to call around to all the pharmacies to try to find this particular drug. Everywhere she called, the answer was always the same. "Madam, this drug is very rare. You can only get it at the regional hospitals and some big private clinics." It was a new drug.

Rebecca looked at the situation and said, "I can't really go to a doctor and say, 'Here's my dream prescription. Would you fill it please?'" So she said, "I'll let this be." She'd wait for God's own time. She went about her life and practically forgot about the dream.

Then one morning she awoke with a

terrible toothache. Her gums were swollen, and it felt as if her teeth were going to fall out. Rebecca got permission from her supervisor at work to go see a dentist at the dental clinic. When she got there, the dentist looked at her teeth. "You've got quite an infection," he said. "I'm going to give you a prescription." He mentioned the name of the medication, and it was exactly the same drug that the doctor in the dream state had prescribed—a very new, rare drug.

Rebecca went home with her prescription, and before the bottle was used up, she was pregnant. Her child is now a little over seven years old. For Rebecca, this experience was proof that the MAHANTA was listening, that the MAHANTA is always with her.

It Helps to Ask

If you want something from life, first of all you have to earn it. But you also have to be open to the gifts life is willing to give you, and that means you have to ask for them.

All too often we don't like to ask.

It never hurts to ask, because somebody just might say yes.

Life might say yes too. A lot of times the bounties of the Holy Spirit are held back from us simply because we don't ask. We want something to come into our life, and we just sit around and wait.

But if you ask for it, be sure you know what you're asking for. You may have to earn it, even the hard way; but by asking, at least you have opened the door. And if it is not for your well-being, the Holy Spirit, in Its infinite wisdom, will help you to know in some way that this is not for you.

By making a request, you put it into the ECK, but then you have to take the steps to figure out what you must do to earn it.

A Spiritual Exercise
for Dream Awareness

$\mathcal{E}$very evening at bedtime, visualize a golden cup to be filled with your dream experiences. The cup sits by your bed.

When you awake in the morning, in contemplation or in your imagination, drink from the cup. You are drinking in the experiences—a conscious way of saying, I want to remember what I'm doing on the inner planes while my body is asleep.

The golden cup is Soul; it is you. As you put more attention on drinking from the cup, it takes on a life of its own. The more the ECK flows in and out of the cup, the more Soul shines of Its own golden light. You, as

Soul, become an ever brighter vehicle for the Holy Spirit.

The experiences you have will lead to greater awareness of your life and its divine meaning.

How Guidance Works

*T*he MAHANTA, the Living ECK Master and the other ECK Masters work with those of you who have an agreement with the Holy Spirit along the lines of the teachings of ECK.

A couple had just bought a new home. The movers were coming on Saturday. On Thursday, the wife called up the movers to confirm. "We're still on for Saturday?" she asked. The people said, "Yes, you're still on for Saturday. We'll bring the truck and two people to help you."

On Saturday, she confirmed again in the morning. The company said, "Yeah, the movers will be out there." So she and her husband sat in their home, surrounded by boxes, waiting. When it got to be twelve thirty and nobody had come, the woman called the moving company again. The voice-mail recording said, "We close at noon on Saturday." They waited until one thirty. Nobody came.

She asked the MAHANTA, "Is this all going to work out OK?" And the MAHANTA said, "Trust. Everything will be OK."

She started calling around. It was Saturday at three o'clock in the afternoon, not a great time to be finding movers. The first two places she called didn't exactly laugh, but there was nobody to help her.

The third call was the charm. On the third ring, somebody picked up the phone and yelled to somebody else in the back room, "Hey, do you want to do another job?" The voice in the back said, "OK." Fifteen minutes later, two movers arrived with their truck. They moved everything very professionally, and they were cheerful. It was late Saturday afternoon, and they were cheerful.

When the other office opened, she talked with them, and they apologized. They even let the couple keep the moving boxes without a charge.

The woman realized that when her plans for Saturday went wrong, she could have become very upset at the first group of movers. But she would've shut down the love channel inside herself. She would have shut off this help from the Inner Master, the MAHANTA. So she kept it open. But she didn't just trust to chance that somehow everything would take care of itself; she got the Yellow Pages and started calling. She didn't stop on the first or second call. She went on to the third.

That's how it works with the Inner Master. You ask for guidance and direction, but then you do what you have to do. Fifty percent is with the Inner Master, and 50 percent is with you.

Your Lifeline to Inner Guidance

*Y*ou are the captain of your own ship; you have the most to gain or lose from its condition.

But you are not at sea alone. The ECK and the MAHANTA offer every guidance to keep you off the rocks and destruction. Whenever you need to boost your confidence, do a Spiritual Exercise of ECK.

It is a lifeline.

The real heart of my message to you is an affirmation of all the opportunities in your life to grow spiritually. Seize the moment; seize the hour; seize the day. Glory in the fact that you are a spark of divine creativity.

All human conditions allow a chance to try your wings, to explore the places that the ECK Masters call home.

Let the ECK and the MAHANTA be your guide in all things.

Following Your Nudges

When you reach a certain level of spiritual unfoldment, you are actually near the forefront of those who are walking the spiritual path. The only one walking with you now is the Inner Master, whose voice is very subtle. You have to learn to listen carefully for the instructions—when to go left, go right, halt, or advance at double time.

The instructions given by the Inner Master are perceived as nudges, feelings, or intuition. Sometimes they come as direct experiences through the dream state, via Soul Travel, or in any number of different ways.

When you listen to them, you know directly what steps to take in order to get through that level of unfoldment.

The farther you go, the fewer maps are available to chart the path. There are fewer travelers. There are fewer players to tell you what to look for, what to watch out for. It is up to you to keep your eyes wide open and stay alert to the guidance of the ECK.

You can no longer rely on memory and established patterns. The rules change so quickly that you can only go by your inner direction.

A Way of Life

This is the way of life for the individual on the path home to God. This is also what makes the path of ECK different from many other religions.

ECK is actually the path of life. We want to know what to do with our life to make it worth the trouble.

What makes this life meaningful? Why is today more meaningful than yesterday? What is the purpose of all the little things that occur?

In ECK we live an active life. We may not know what tomorrow will bring, but it doesn't matter; we try to do the best we can today with the spiritual insight that we have gained through the Spiritual Exercises of ECK.

Creativity and Imagination

A woman recently had a brush with death after she became ill with toxic shock syndrome. The disease began to get the better of her. At one point, her feet became numb, her blood pressure fell to a dangerous level, and the pain was nearly beyond endurance.

A team of young doctors set to work to save her life.

The night her illness reached a crisis, she felt very afraid of sleep. She thought it necessary to stay awake to survive, and that night proved to be the longest of her life. To make it till morning, she made up a Spiritual Exercise of ECK. She imagined herself in the company of the MAHANTA

35

(the Inner Master) and other ECK friends. She saw herself relaxing in their arms. The exercise was simplicity itself.

Later she made up other exercises that included HU, an ancient name for God, which she sang repeatedly.

The night passed, and the illness with it. This crisis brought her a realization about the Spiritual Exercises of ECK: It took a real effort to create them during this emergency. She then realized the value of doing them daily before the onset of trouble.

Waiting until the hour of desperation could be too late. As it was, it still took her a lot of imagination and effort to create them during the pain of her illness. But her daily practice of the spiritual exercises had made it easier to reach for the love and support of the MAHANTA and other ECK Initiates.

The experience was a crossroads for her. In the future, she plans to give up several negative traits that have held her back spiritually and put more energy into higher ambitions. It's a far better response to the Voice of God.

God is always speaking to us and all life through the Holy Spirit.

Listen to God's Voice. Respond to It spiritually and know that, despite every appearance to the contrary, all is well and in its rightful place.

WAKING DREAMS AND GOLDEN-TONGUED WISDOM

*I*nner guidance can also come in the form of a waking dream or through Golden-tongued Wisdom. These are two different categories of experience.

Sometimes it is hard to tell which is which. Whereas the waking dream usually involves some kind of action in the outer world, the Golden-tongued Wisdom normally involves voice.

The Golden-tongued Wisdom is the voice of the MAHANTA that jumps out to impart spiritual insight. It might come through words spoken by another person, or even in a short printed message. The

Golden-tongued Wisdom is usually an outer experience, but it may also come on the inner planes.

These works are all a part of you.

But the ECK can come so quietly that we often overlook the message It carries: how to protect ourselves and avoid unnecessary problems. We overlook the message because our state of consciousness hasn't quite expanded into the next circle of awareness. But when it does, we then get a bigger picture of life and a better idea of how the ECK is talking to us.

When your inner feeling says, How about going left here a couple of steps, then right, then two more to the left? it's the ECK, or the MAHANTA, trying to guide you through life. And because you are being guided by the spiritual power, you will be led in a better direction than the highest degree of reasoning could ever hope to steer you.

In California they once had a series of rainstorms. It rained so heavily, in fact, that you couldn't even drive in the daytime without the headlights turned on. On one of these rainy days, "Nancy," an ECKist, went to visit a friend. Unfortunately, she didn't have one of the cars that beeps or talks to you when you leave your lights on.

As she pulled into the driveway of her friend's apartment building, she noticed a yellow tow truck parked out on the street. The driver sat there, looking around strangely. She thought there might be something wrong with him.

After she parked her car, the image of the tow truck stayed with her. It was such a strong feeling that she walked back out to the street to see if the tow truck was still there. It was.

Nancy forgot about the tow truck as she visited with her friend for several hours. But when she got in her car to drive home, the engine wouldn't turn over at all—the battery was dead. She had forgotten to turn off the car lights. She then had to go through the inconvenience of finding someone to jump-start her car. It wasn't until the next day that it occurred to her the ECK had been trying to give her a message.

Rainstorms present an unusual condition for Californians. Nancy had to drive with the lights on in the daytime, and she wasn't used to it, which means she also wasn't used to shutting the lights off.

Because the ECK works in every area of life, It tried to find a way to tell her to shut off the lights. In this case, it brought a truck—a yellow tow truck. This is an example of the waking dream, which is another form of the Golden-tongued Wisdom.

You start with a certain degree of consciousness. It then begins to expand in concentric circles around you. As it reaches out farther and farther, you encompass more of the knowledge that you need to make better decisions so that your life runs better. Every time you're on the wrong track, the ECK will try to tell you that something is amiss.

Let Your Viewpoint Be Centered in Spirit

In all things it is to our advantage to listen to the ECK, a sure guide.

Will all then go "right"? If your viewpoint is housed in the human consciousness, you will appear to win out over some quandaries but lose out to others. Let your viewpoint be centered in the spiritual realm, however, and you realize that every experience is for your good. The ECK is giving you vital experiences to expand your state of consciousness.

The Master says, "I am always with you." There is never any need to panic and say, Why have you forsaken me? The love of the Master is always there, and it takes only our acceptance and our awareness of it.

I might mention that we don't look to the ECK to take care of our daily problems and our daily situations. We do what we can, we put ourselves into it 100 percent, and then the ECK smoothes the way wherever needed. Wherever the ditch gets too wide to jump across, It might lead you to a bridge.

A man wrote to report an incident that had happened to his wife, "Zina," where she had received the protection of the ECK in her daily life. This took place in another country where there is less freedom and it's easier for the military forces to control people or take them into custody than it is here. This family is not wealthy, and every day the wife would go to the shipyard, buy fish, clean and smoke them, and then resell them. In this way she was able to add a little to the household finances.

This particular day, as usual, Zina went

to buy and sell the fish, when the naval patrol came through and made a lightning raid on the wharf, pulling in a lot of the hawkers and people who were changing foreign currency, which was illegal. Selling fish was not illegal, but the arm of the law in that country isn't very particular until they get you down to the police station to interrogate you and find out who belonged there and who didn't.

These people were taken to the naval-patrol station, where they were interrogated and some were beaten.

Zina wasn't beaten, but she was interrogated.

When she started to chant *HU*, an ancient and sacred name of God, quietly and inwardly, the Inner Master gave her the nudge to call her husband's name out loud.

She wondered, *Why should I be calling my husband's name when I ought to be calling the name of one of the ECK Masters?* But she listened to the nudge, followed it without question, and started chanting her husband's name.

All of a sudden one of the naval men walked up to her and said, "Why are you calling my name?" She said, "I was calling my husband's name. I haven't eaten all day, and I'm getting very dizzy." He then reached into his pocket and took some money out. He said, "Here, take this money, go to our naval canteen right over there, and get yourself something to eat."

So she took the money and went across the room to the naval canteen to get herself some food.

Zina was also very bright. She happened to look outside the door just then, and she saw a taxicab sitting there with the door open. Without even a backward glance, she walked outside, got into the cab, and shut the door. The cab took off.

She said the reason they didn't pursue

her was because the other naval personnel had seen this naval man talking to her and giving her money. They just assumed she must be a relative.

She felt this very definitely was help from the Inner Master, but she had to use her own common sense too. When you see a taxicab with the door open, get in!

An Unexpected Gift

"*Lucy*" discovered how a simple nudge could guide her to turn a looming disaster into a joyous occasion.

Lucy's daughter had used illegal drugs. The girl was thirteen, and her explorations had landed her in a drug rehabilitation program, where she spent most of her day and had her schooling. It was now just before Thanksgiving Day. Lucy was a volunteer with the rehab program, and the staff knew her. So they agreed to let six of the rehab youth come to Lucy's home for Thanksgiving dinner.

Then, a cloud on the horizon. Her boyfriend at the time, "Ron," dropped in while Lucy and her three kids were preparing dinner. He had brought a folding table at which to seat everyone.

A word about Ron: He was usually a good-hearted person. But a veteran of Vietnam, he had physical and mental scars, which sometimes caused him to fly into a rage at the least provocation. Some little annoyance lit his fuse that day.

Very angry, he shouted at the top of his lungs and pulled the tablecloth from the table, hurling the silverware onto the floor. Ron then folded up his table and stormed out the door, slamming it shut behind him.

Silence. Total, shocked silence.

Oh, great! thought Lucy. *What now?*

A nudge came that she later realized had come to her from the MAHANTA, the Inner Master. Why not, he said, turn this potential disaster into a special event?

With a smile, she broke the silence.

"OK, now on to Plan B," she said. "Kids, we are going to have some fun!" She ran to the linen closet, placed a large bedsheet on the floor, put the tablecloth on it, then made an announcement. "This is our new table."

So they brought all the food down on the tablecloth and sat cross-legged to eat.

Then Lucy said to them, "We not only have this opportunity to enjoy our dinner, to be grateful for each other's company, and to be grateful for the blessings in our lives, but the Holy Spirit has given us an unexpected gift today that we can take with us for the rest of our lives. And because this gift was given to us in such a dramatic way, I expect none of us will forget it."

The Inner Master, who is spiritually akin to the Holy Spirit, prompted Lucy to say a few more words to her six visitors. Most were from troubled homes.

"This is the gift," she continued. "If someone ever tries to take the table from under you, always have another place to put the tablecloth and go on with your life. Don't allow someone else's bitterness or anger to take the peace and the love from your heart.

"In life, we don't have much control over what other people will say or do, or how they will behave, but we do have control of how we understand it and let it affect us."

That immediately changed the mood in the room. The youth began to tell how, in the past, they had let other people's attitudes affect how they felt about themselves.

Lucy noticed a healing taking place. It was a feeling of being on holy ground, a feeling she would notice many times over in the future as a member of Eckankar. It occurs when someone invites the ECK, the Holy Spirit, into a situation to handle it. The atmosphere inside and outside one changes.

So much had the mood lifted, in fact,

that the group raised their apple-juice glasses in a toast to Ron.

"We hope you can let your anger cool and also enjoy your Thanksgiving!" This toast and spirit of forgiveness was quite a marvelous step for these youth, whose parents may have been on drugs, fighting each other, or just not around.

The evening had turned out much better than Lucy could ever have imagined.

Yet there was a lingering concern. What would happen when the youth shared their Thanksgiving-dinner experience with the rehabilitation staff? Would they ever trust her again to provide a safe environment for the kids?

But Lucy had worried for nothing.

The youth, it turned out, were more impressed with how they had shifted gears than with the actual disruption.

And when it came right down to it, one of the rehab counselors thought that Lucy had probably staged the disruption to give the young people this experience. But that was hardly the case.

Lucy observed that after she joined Eckankar, the answers often came readily whenever she asked.

That Thanksgiving Day, she now realized, she had asked, and the MAHANTA had answered. It was as simple as that.

INNER GUIDANCE ON YOUR
JOURNEY HOME TO GOD

*L*ight and Sound, just like the rain and the wind, come to everyone equally and alike. But some people benefit more than others.

It's up to you in your state of consciousness.

And your state of consciousness depends upon whether or not you care enough to open yourself to this inner guidance of Divine Spirit so that you can have some of the experiences that are necessary to break through this hard human shell.

The search for God requires a deep yearning. Soul hears the Voice of God and wants to return to Its home in heaven. In the meantime, it's up to Soul, in one way or another, to find a path that gives the help It needs to take this step.

When you graduate from one level of education in the spiritual works, God provides a step, then another and another.

Find Something for Yourself That Works

No matter what path you are on or what faith you follow, be the best there is in it; be the cream of the crop. Because until you are that, you haven't learned the lessons that you need to learn; and until they are learned, you will not be able to graduate to the next step and learn the greater truth.

I will leave you with this. And if there is some little thing I've said that makes you think maybe there is something to it—maybe you don't agree but you've decided to look further on your own—then through this, you might find something for yourself that works. It may not be the path of ECK. But through your efforts, you will be doing something important for yourself.

You will have gotten off the seat, stood up, looked around, and made this decision: I want to find this path to God and walk it for myself.

A SPIRITUAL EXERCISE TO MEET THE MAHANTA

Take a comfortable sitting position on your bed or in a chair. Gaze gently and sweetly into the Spiritual Eye between the eyebrows.

Everything may appear dark for a moment. Gaze into the space between the brows. Look for the Light, a sheet of white light.

The Light may be like a great sun, throwing Its glittering, brilliant rays in a circle around you. Its brilliancy greater than ten thousand suns.

Suddenly you realize that the Light is coming from within yourself, spreading into an ever-widening circle until It fills the whole universe. It flows out of a center within you and becomes a burning beacon.

Feel your whole body pulse with the rhythm of Its surging waves like the pounding of surf upon a sandy beach.

You hear the roaring of the surf in your ears, and it grows and grows. Suddenly into your inner vision steps the MAHANTA, the Living ECK Master.

Greet him with joy in your heart, and begin your journey into the worlds of God.

NEXT STEPS IN
SPIRITUAL EXPLORATION

- **Try a spiritual exercise.**
  Review the spiritual exercises in this book.
  Experiment with them.

- **Browse our website: www.Eckankar.org.**
  Watch videos; get free books, answers to
  FAQs, and more info.

- **Attend an Eckankar event** in your area.
  Visit "Find a Location" (under "Engage") on
  our website.

- **Enroll** in an ECK Advanced Spiritual Living
  course.

- **Read additional books** about the ECK
  teachings.

- **Call us:** Call 1-800-LOVE GOD (1-800-568-
  3463, toll-free, automated) or (952) 380-2222
  (direct).

- **Write to:** ECKANKAR, Dept. BK127, PO Box
  2000, Chanhassen, MN 55317-2000 USA.

FOR FURTHER READING
By Harold Klemp

The Spiritual Exercises of ECK

This book is a staircase with 131 steps leading to the doorway to spiritual freedom, self-mastery, wisdom, and love. A comprehensive volume of spiritual exercises for every need.

ECK Wisdom on Conquering Fear

Would having more courage and confidence help you make the most of this lifetime?

Going far beyond typical self-help advice, this book invites you to explore divine love as the antidote to anxiety and the doorway to inner freedom.

You will discover ways

to identify the karmic roots of fear and align with your highest ideals.

Use this book to soar beyond your limitations and reap the benefits of self-mastery.

Live life to its fullest potential!

ECK Wisdom on Dreams

This dream study will help you be more *awake* than you've ever been!

ECK Wisdom on Dreams reveals the most ancient of dream teachings for a richer and more productive life today.

In this dynamic book, author Harold Klemp shows you how to remember your dreams, apply dream wisdom to everyday situations, recognize prophetic dreams, and more.

You will be introduced to the art of dream interpretation and offered techniques to discover the treasures of your inner worlds.

ECK Wisdom on Health and Healing

This book is rich with spiritual keys to better health on every level.

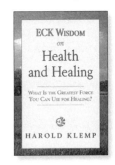

Discover the spiritual roots of illness and how gratitude can open your heart to God's love and healing.

Simple spiritual exercises go deep to help you get personal divine guidance and insights.

Revitalize your connection with the true healing power of God's love.

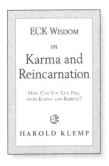

ECK Wisdom on Karma and Reincarnation

Have you lived before? What is the real meaning of life?

Discover your divine destiny—to move beyond the limits of karma and reincarnation and gain spiritual freedom.

This book reveals the purpose of living and the keys to spiritual growth.

You'll find answers to age-old questions about fate, destiny, and free will. These gems of wisdom can enhance your relationships, health, and happiness—and offer the chance to resolve all your karma in this lifetime!

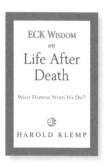

ECK Wisdom on Life after Death

All that lies ahead is already within your heart.

ECK Wisdom on Life after Death invites you to explore the eternal nature of *you!*

Author Harold Klemp offers you new perspectives on seeing heaven before you die, meeting with departed loved ones, near-death experiences, getting help from spiritual guides, animals in heaven, and dealing with grief.

Try the techniques and spiritual exercise included in this book to find answers and explore the secrets of life after death—for yourself.

ECK Wisdom on Prayer, Meditation, and Contemplation

Bring balance and wonder to your life!

This book is a portal to your direct, personal connection with Divine Spirit.

Harold Klemp shows how you can experience the powerful benefits of contemplation—"a conversation with the most secret, most genuine, and most mysterious part of yourself."

Move beyond traditional meditation via dynamic spiritual exercises. Learn about the uplifting chant of HU (an ancient holy name for God), visualization, creative imagination, and other active techniques.

ECK Wisdom on Relationships

Find the answers to common questions of the heart, including the truth about soul mates, how to strengthen a marriage, and how to know if a partnership is worth developing.

The spiritual exercises included in this book can help you break a pattern of poor relationships and find balance. You'll learn new ways to open your heart to love and enrich your relationship with God.

This book is a key for anyone wanting more love to give, more love to get. It's a key to better relationships with everyone in your life.

ECK Wisdom on Solving Problems

Problems? Problems! Why do we have so many? What causes them? Can we avoid them?

Author Harold Klemp, the spiritual leader of Eckankar, can help you answer these questions and more. His sense of humor and practical approach offer spiritual keys to unlock the secrets to effective problem solving. Learn creative, time-tested techniques to

- find the root cause of a problem;
- change your viewpoint and overcome difficulties;
- conquer your fears;
- work beyond symptoms to solutions;

- kindle your creativity;
- master your karma, past and present;
- receive spiritual guidance that can transform the way you see yourself and your life.

ECK Wisdom on Soul Travel

Where do you go when you close your eyes?

Nowhere? Are you sure?

What about when you daydream?

You go places, don't you?

What about when you close your eyes at night—and dream? When dreams seem more real than everyday life?

That's Soul Travel. It's a natural process that opens the door to the incredible universes where we truly live and have our being. You are Soul, a divine spark of God. The more attention you give to this wonderful truth, the closer you get to the very heart of God.

You learn how to grow in love and awareness. And that's what life is all about, isn't it?

ECK Wisdom on Soul Travel gives you tools to experiment with and introduces you to a spiritual guide who can show you the road to your infinite future—a road that courses through every moment of your daily life.

Take a peek, and explore your own adventure of a lifetime!

ECK Wisdom on Spiritual Freedom

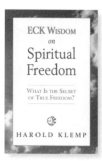

Are you everything you want to be? You came into this life to spread your wings and live in freedom—heart, mind, and Soul!

Author Harold Klemp puts the tools of spiritual freedom firmly in your grasp:

- Keys to embrace the highest expression of who you really are
- Techniques to tap into the divine Life Force for unlimited creativity and problem solving
- New paradigms to reveal the power of loving yourself, God, and all of life

What would you give for the secret of true freedom? Consider this book a ticket to an unexpected destination—the heart of your being.

Open your wings, and prepare for flight!

The Call of Soul

Discover how to find spiritual freedom in this lifetime and the infinite world of God's love for you. Includes a CD with dream and Soul Travel techniques.

Past Lives, Dreams, and Soul Travel

These stories and exercises help you find your true purpose, discover greater love than you've ever known, and learn that spiritual freedom is within reach.

The MAHANTA Transcripts Series

The MAHANTA Transcripts, books 1–18, are from Harold Klemp's talks at Eckankar seminars. He has taught thousands how to have a natural, direct relationship with the Holy Spirit. The stories and wonderful insights contained in these talks will lead you to deeper spiritual understanding.

Autobiography of a Modern Prophet

This riveting story of Harold Klemp's climb up the Mountain of God will help you discover the keys to your own spiritual greatness.

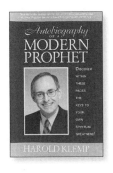

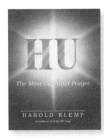

HU, the Most Beautiful Prayer

Singing *HU*, the ancient name for God, can open your heart and lead you to a new understanding of yourself. Includes a CD of the HU Song.

Those Wonderful ECK Masters

Would you like to have *personal* experience with spiritual Masters that people all over the world—since the beginning of time—have looked to for guidance, protection, and divine love? This book includes real-life stories and spiritual exercises to meet eleven ECK Masters.

The Sound of Soul

Sacred Sound, ancient mantra. HU is a universal love song to God; It brings alignment with your true purpose and highest good. This potent volume of contemplation seeds and spiritual exercises can get you started on the journey of a lifetime—your return to the heart of God.

GLOSSARY

Words set in SMALL CAPS are defined elsewhere in this glossary.

Blue Light   How the MAHANTA often appears in the inner worlds to the CHELA or seeker.

chela   A spiritual student of ECKANKAR.

ECK   The Life Force, Holy Spirit, or Audible Life Current which sustains all life.

Eckankar *EHK-ahn-kahr*   The Path of Spiritual Freedom. Also known as the Ancient Science of SOUL TRAVEL. A truly spiritual way of life for the individual in modern times. The teachings provide a framework for anyone to explore their own spiritual experiences. Established by PAUL TWITCHELL, the modern-day founder, in 1965. The word means Coworker with God.

ECK Masters   Spiritual Masters who can assist and protect people in their spiritual studies and travels. The ECK Masters are from a long line of God-Realized SOULS who know the responsibility that goes with spiritual freedom.

71

God-Realization   The state of God Consciousness. Complete and conscious awareness of God. To love as God loves.

HU   *HYOO*   The most ancient, secret name for God. It can be sung as a love song to God aloud or silently to oneself to align with God's love.

Karma, Law of   The Law of Cause and Effect, action and reaction, justice, retribution, and reward, which applies to the lower or psychic worlds: the Physical, Astral, Causal, Mental, and Etheric PLANES.

Klemp, Harold   The present MAHANTA, the LIVING ECK MASTER. SRI Harold Klemp became the MAHANTA, the Living ECK Master in 1981. His spiritual name is WAH Z.

Living ECK Master   The spiritual leader of ECKANKAR. He leads SOUL back to God. He teaches in the physical world as the Outer Master, in the dream state as the Dream Master, and in the spiritual worlds as the Inner Master. SRI HAROLD KLEMP became the MAHANTA, the Living ECK Master in 1981.

MAHANTA   An expression of the Spirit of God that is always with you. Sometimes seen as the BLUE LIGHT or Blue Star or in the form of the MAHANTA, the LIVING ECK MASTER. The highest state of God Consciousness on earth, only embodied in the Living ECK Master. He is the Living Word.

planes Levels of existence, such as the Physical, Astral, Causal, Mental, Etheric, and SOUL Planes.

Self-Realization SOUL recognition. The entering of Soul into the Soul PLANE and there beholding Itself as pure Spirit. A state of Seeing, Knowing, and Being.

Shariyat-Ki-Sugmad Way of the Eternal; the sacred scriptures of ECKANKAR. The scriptures are comprised of twelve volumes in the spiritual worlds. The first two were transcribed from the inner PLANES by PAUL TWITCHELL, modern-day founder of Eckankar.

Soul The True Self, an individual, eternal spark of God. The inner, most sacred part of each person. Soul can see, know, and perceive all things. It is the creative center of Its own world.

Soul Travel The expansion of consciousness. The ability of SOUL to transcend the physical body and travel into the spiritual worlds of God. Soul Travel is taught only by the LIVING ECK MASTER. It helps people unfold spiritually and can provide proof of the existence of God and life after death.

Sound and Light of ECK The Holy Spirit. The two aspects through which God appears in the lower worlds. People can experience them by looking and listening within themselves and through SOUL TRAVEL.

Spiritual Exercises of ECK Daily practices for direct, personal experience with the God Current. Creative techniques using contemplation and the singing of sacred words to bring the higher awareness of SOUL into daily life.

Sri A title of spiritual respect, similar to reverend or pastor, used for those who have attained the Kingdom of God. In ECKANKAR, it is reserved for the MAHANTA, the LIVING ECK MASTER.

SUGMAD *SOOG-mahd* A sacred name for God. It is the source of all life, neither male nor female, the Ocean of Love and Mercy.

Temples of Golden Wisdom Golden Wisdom Temples found on the various PLANES—from the Physical to the Anami Lok; CHELAS of ECKANKAR are taken to these temples in the SOUL body to be educated in the divine knowledge; sections of the SHARIYAT-KI-SUGMAD, the sacred teachings of ECK, are kept at these temples.

Twitchell, Paul An American ECK Master who brought the modern teachings of ECKANKAR to the world through his writings and lectures. His spiritual name is Peddar Zaskq.

Wah Z *WAH zee* The spiritual name of SRI HAROLD KLEMP. It means the secret doctrine. It is his name in the spiritual worlds.

For more explanations of ECKANKAR terms, see *A Cosmic Sea of Words: The ECKANKAR Lexicon*, by Harold Klemp.

ABOUT THE AUTHOR

Award-winning author, teacher, and spiritual guide Sri Harold Klemp helps seekers reach their full potential.

He is the MAHANTA, the Living ECK Master and spiritual leader of Eckankar, the Path of Spiritual Freedom. He is the latest in a long line of spiritual Adepts who have served throughout history in every culture of the world.

Sri Harold teaches creative spiritual practices that enable anyone to achieve life mastery and gain inner peace and contentment. His messages are relevant to today's spiritual needs and resonate with every generation.

Sri Harold's body of work includes more than one hundred books, which have been translated into eighteen languages and won multiple awards. The miraculous, true-life stories he shares lift the veil between heaven and earth.

In his groundbreaking memoir, *Autobiography of a Modern Prophet,* he reveals secrets to spiritual success gleaned from his personal journey into the heart of God.

Find your own path to true happiness, wisdom, and love in Sri Harold Klemp's inspired writings.